All That Might Be Done

Books by Samuel Green

Gillnets // Cold Mountain Press

Wind // Breakwater Press

Hands Learning to Work // Brooding Heron Press

Vertebrae // Grey Spider Press

Keeping Faith // Grey Spider Press

Communion // Grey Spider Press

Vertebrae: Poems 1978-1994 //
Eastern Washington University Press

Working in the Dark // Grey Spider Press

The Only Time We Have // Grey Spider Press

The Grace of Necessity // Carnegie Mellon University Press
(Winner of the Washington State Book
Award for Poetry)

First Up: Barnstorming for Poetry // Chuckanut Editions,
Village Books

All That Might Be Done // Carnegie Mellon University Press

All That Might Be Done

Samuel Green

Carnegie Mellon University Press
Pittsburgh 2014

Acknowledgments

Many of these poems have appeared in the following anthologies and periodicals:

Fragments; Puerto del Sol; Alaska Quarterly Review; Crosscurrents; Seattle Woman; Mountains Moving; Tri-County Herald; Vietnam Veterans Newsletter; Clover (Volumes 3, 4, & 5); *Conversations Across Borders; Journal of Comparative and Continental Philosophy; Virginia Quarterly Review; The Moment Witnessed* (Skagit River Poetry Festival Anthology, 2008); *Into the Open* (Skagit River Poetry Festival Anthology, 2010); *Drawn to the Light* (Skagit River Poetry Festival Anthology, 2012); *Poems from Planet Earth* (Leaf Press, 2013); *New Poets of the American West* (Many Voices Press, 2010); *Red Thread, Gold Thread* (Power of Poetry, 2009); *An Endless Skyway: Poetry from the State Poets Laureate* (Ice Cube Books, 2011); *Ghost Town Poetry* (Cover to Cover Books, 2010); *First Up* (Village Books, 2012).

"Tulip Field, McLean Road" was issued as a letterpressed broadside by Wood-Works Press.
"Stroke" was issued as a broadside by Egress Press.

Book design by Jean Kwon

Library of Congress Control Number 2013937536
ISBN 978-0-88748-582-4 Signed limited clothbound edition
ISBN 978-0-88748-581-7 Pbk.
Copyright © 2014 by Samuel Green
All rights reserved
Printed and bound in the United States of America

10 9 8 7 6 5 4 3 2 1

for Sally, wife, life partner

for Cora, our beloved granddaughter

&

in memoriam

Hayden Carruth, William Kloefkorn, John Haines,

John O'Leary, Dennis O'Driscoll, Kathleene West, Judith Kleck

&

Phyllis Ennes

The author wishes to thank: the editors who first published so many of these poems; the National Endowment for the Arts for a Fellowship in Poetry which provided support during which many of these poems were written; Artist Trust of Washington for a Fellowship in Literature; the Washington State Arts Commission and Humanities Washington for support during tenure as the State of Washington's Inaugural Poet Laureate (2008-2010); Edwin Weihe and colleagues at Seattle University; the administrators & teachers connected with the Skagit River Poetry Project; Gerald Costanzo and Cynthia Lamb at Carnegie Mellon University Press; the Washington Center for the Book. Thanks also to the following for crucial advice and/or continuing encouragement: Donald Hall, Hayden Carruth, Joe-Anne McLaughlin, Paul Hunter, Tony Curtis, Theo Dorgan, Paula Meehan, Joseph Powell, Lorraine Ferra, Tim McNulty, Michael Daley, Phyllis Ennes, Morten Lauridsen, Ted Kooser, Barry Sternlieb, Lonny Kaneko, David Lee, Bill Ransom, Sean McDowell, William O'Daly, Rachel Rose, Alice Derry, Kim Stafford. Sally remains the keystone.

. . . so we do hope to heare the sweete callings of the daye,

but the feerce birde of memorie insists, & drives them all awaye

—anon.

Contents

I

Grandmother, Cleaning a Rabbit

I shot this one by the upper pond of the farm
after watching the rings trout made rising
to flies, watching small birds pace the backs
of cows, hoping all the time it would run.

My grandmother told me they damaged her garden.

I think it was a way to make the killing
lighter. She never let me clean them, only asked
I bring them headless to her. I bring this one
to the fir block near the house, use the single-
bitted axe with the nick in the lower crescent
of the blade, smell the slow fire
in the smokehouse, salmon changing
to something sweet & dark. A fly turns
in a bead of blood on my boot. I tuck
the head in a hole beside the dusty globes
of ripened currants, talk quiet to the barn cat.

In her kitchen my grandmother whets the thin blade
of her Barlow, makes a series of quick, clever cuts, then tugs
off the skin like a child's sweater. This one was
pregnant. She pulls out a row of unborn rabbits
like the sleeve of a shirt with a series of knots.
The offal is dropped in a bucket. Each joint gives way
beneath her knife as though it wants
to come undone, as though she knows some secret
about how things fit together. I have killed
a hundred rabbits since I was eight.

This will be the last.

I am twenty, & about to go back
to the war that killed my cousin in *Kien Hoa*,
which is one more name she can't pronounce.
I haven't told her about the dead
& she won't ask. She rolls the meat
in flour & pepper & salt & lays it
in a skillet of oil that spits like a cat.
She cannot save a single boy who carries a gun.
All she can do is feed this one.

Stroke

Where is the axe, says the ice in the trough, left in the field for the cows.
    Here, says the file on the bench in the shed stuck in a hole by the vise.
Where is the cup with a chip in its rim, says the sink with its saucer & spoon.
    Here, says the kitchen linoleum square, in fragments the color of bone.
Where is the milk, says the pail on the porch, scalded & shining & worn.
    Here, say the bells of the shuffling heifers stalled at the door of the barn.
Where is the cream for the cinnamon cat, says the tuna can under the stairs.
    Here, says a shelf in the cold-box, with the butter & leftover pears.
Where is the heat for the dinner, say the skillet & pans on the range.
    Here, say the split chunks of alder & fir, carefully dried & arranged.
Where is the ball made of leftover twine, says the unfinished rug on the stool.
    Here, says the awkward crochet hook made from an old-fashioned nail.
Where is the woman who lives in this house, says the work coat still hung on a chair.
    Here, says the wind through the grass of the field,
    here say the waves on the bay past the bluff,
    here says the breath in the air.
Not here, say the cows, *not here*, says the cat, *not here*, say the boots by the door.
Not here, says the stove, *not here*, says the coat, *not here*, says the shape on the floor.

My Father Burns His Mother's Underwear

He knows how to make a fire in December
rain: orchard trimmings from a dozen pear
& apple trees, dried canes of raspberries she left
in bundles bound with baling twine, old cedar posts
saved for kindling, a cup of kerosene
from the lamp on the fridge. He has built it just
beyond the farmhouse on the path
the cows took morning & evening on their way
to the barn, their dull bells clanging.

I am watching from her kitchen window, wiping
the few odd dishes left on the counter. My father has rolled
up the sleeves of his shirt, green-checked flannel
crossed with red suspenders that clip to his jeans.
His beard is the color of fresh milk
in a bucket. He turns from the smoke
to face the bay beneath the bluff, a tug with a log raft
in tow, moving south against the tide. He puts
a thumb in his mouth, scrapes something
from a tooth, then rubs his temples
the way I used to watch him worry
grease into a pair of leather boots
to keep them supple. He looks

nothing like the boy who ran from his father
on butchering days, away from the stink of the hog
hung from a singletree, scalded bristles, the whiskey
in his father's voice. He hid behind a curtain
of honeysuckle where it fell from the top
of a cedar stump. He stood, he said, still

as a veal calf while the hummingbirds came
to the flame-orange blossoms, came
right at his eyes, inches
away, their long thin tongues curling out
& into the sweet flutes.

In a moment he will bend & lift a box filled
from his mother's drawers: her bras, old-woman
underpants, a few dark pair of pantyhose, elastic
bandages she wrapped around her legs
each morning. When he dumps it out the smoke will boil
toward the white page of sky like spilled ink.
Then he will burn the box. He will watch the fire wear
itself out while ash gathers like snow on his shoulders
& cinders eat holes in his hat. Back in her kitchen, he will sit
at the table with coffee she did not make. He will wipe
a wet smudge of ash from his forehead with a dab of spit
& a blue cotton kerchief. There will be a small scratch
on the inside of his right wrist. He will look more
like his dead father than he could ever admit.

For now, he is still standing by the fire, about to do
the last chore he can for his mother, after which
he will become only the grieving boy she's left behind.
He will know there is gone from the world the last
person with answers to questions that will trouble
his mind. In a year, he will say he has no memory
about any of this, will deny it ever took place. And I will be
the son with a stolen square of cotton in a corner
of his drawer because it smells like his father. Wrapped

inside are a pair of scorched metal snaps raked
from the pasture grass. I will be the son who wonders if
such gestures matter, why we cannot let them easily pass.

New Owner

The new owner is sick & tinker-tired,
he says, of all us grandkids stopping by
just to set foot on the land she worked
& walked, & so what if we offer to prune
the orchard the way we know she did,
& why would he care a gnat's eyebrow
where she kept her pitchfork, axe, or rake
& no, we can't check the old henhouse
for fake eggs we played with, or see
if a hidden cowbell is still in the same place,
& he doesn't want to see my initials
& some girl's carved on the bottom of a heart-
grained beam halfway up the weather side
of the barn after she & I slid our itchy bodies
out of the bales, & no, we can't have that hay hook
with the groove her right thumb wore in the handle,
no one should have left it there in the first
damned place, & he wouldn't give two shits
to know where we used to dump the heads & guts
of butchered steers over the bluff, & no,
we can't go look for skulls, & her berries
are long gone, he pulled them out, so don't ask
for starts, & forget about hoping to rake smelt
on the beach, they don't spawn there anymore,
& so what if we used to shoot a lot of rabbits,
there are still a lot, so we didn't make much of a dent
did we, & he couldn't care a starving barn cat's ass
less about the names she gave her cows, & why
can't we realize it's been two dozen years
since she had that stroke & died & none of this

will bring her back, & no, no, no,
he's never wondered whether anyone
anywhere will love him for so long, & like that.

Remembering the Names

He is wondering what happened
to the old names: *Hazel & Alma,*
Esther & Vera, Vivian, Netta
& Gwen. I think he imagines them
appearing again
like heritage apples
in supermarket bins, each
with its own peculiar
scent & savor, sweet or
tart, each with its own
story of ripening,
how he might take them up,
rub them against the soft
flannel of remembrance
until they blush.

Trade Jargon

Great-grandmother, Mora, Washington, 1921

Hazel came home from her job waiting
tables at the Mora Hotel. A pile driving crew
has been taking its meals there. She said
the whole table snickered at noon
when someone mentioned the light

near Cape Flattery: *Tatoosh*. She guessed
they knew what it means in the jargon. She blushed
when she told me. Coarse men, smirking
like boys at the trade word for *breast*. And what
would they know about anything soft? Do they think

we don't see the way they clutch fish, slap the flanks
of a horse, grip the handles of tools? Soft is *klimmin*
in Chinook, a little catch in the throat, & then
the lips & teeth. Some men can make any word
seem like cold grease caught on the roof

of the mouth. When my brother Wesley
ran the reservation school at La Push, I went there,
too. All our games were played in Chinook. I liked
the simple way that meanings braided
together: *tumtum* for heart, its insistent

beat. *Kloshe* for beautiful or beloved—as though
whatever is beautiful must be beloved, whatever
is beloved has beauty. *Kloshe tumtum*: spirit, soul,
great heart. Who wouldn't be charmed? But Wesley thrashed
the children for speaking such words in class

though he used them himself when he bargained
for baskets, for fish, or for labor, quick-tongued
& harsh, as though words were like steam
for bending cedar into a box. Papa & Wesley
seemed always watching. I was *tenas kloochman*:

small girl, virgin. They said my every thought
was heard. I found a deer bed once in the brush
beyond the blueberry patch, a buck by the scent
of the musk, & lay there for an hour out of the sun's
light. *Tenas*: little. *Oly*: cry. A sigh was

tenas oly: small cry. I needed sounds
to understand the sort of rain that hangs
in a patch of ferns, sun shimmering through beach
fog, the smell of fresh-picked morels, the light
shivering of the body. Hazel said the man who'd laughed

loudest at the joke followed her to the barn
when she went to milk the hotel cow. He told her
a woman shouldn't do such work when a man was
around, though all he did was talk
while she filled the bucket, her hands stripping

the teats stream by stream. I tell her—mother
to daughter—that men want words they believe
will send a woman's hands to the buttons
of her dress. They are *halo tumtum*: without
heart, a child without will, mud
inside the bright shell of a clam.

My Mother, Fetching a Switch

By now she knows that just because it's thin
doesn't mean it won't hurt, that green is better
than dead & dried. She needs to choose
between the hot sting of a wasp, or a dull

deep ache that lasts for days, bruises the color
of certain pears when they ripen. There are the canes
of bigleaf maple, willow, alder, the straight suckers
from apple or plum in the orchard. She knows to peel

bark from the wand & shave the nodes flush
to the stem with whatever knife she's given
from pocket or kitchen drawer. Her first switch
left her bloody, then a web of tiny white scars fine

as lace in the doilies her sisters sometimes helped her
make. Once she brought her father a long whip
of pussy willow with the soft toes of catkins
left on. He laughed so hard he let her off. A second try

made him madder. Once she split a thin strip of cedar
from a shake bolt, lighter than lath; her mother used the edge
like a dull blade. She knows to lift her dress waist-
high, overalls unsnapped & dropped

to her ankles. Her father likes her
folded across a single knee & only strikes
the cheeks of her fanny. Her mother takes her
standing, feet apart, & whales at any skin

she sees: calves, her inner thighs. She knows
if she cries or squirms the blows come faster, last
longer, how anger travels into rage. She knows
exactly how long she has to find & shape

& fetch a switch to its waiting hand.
My grandparents think she's learning
the wages of backsass, what happens
when you ride the stubborn donkey of disobedience,

but she is learning how short the pleasure is
when she flushes a rabbit from the brush,
that there isn't quite time to wholly peel
& eat an apple before someone will come

looking for her, that no joy lasts long,
that—father, mother, lover—it is painful
to be alive. All she can do is choose
between one hurt & another.

Plane Song

Always his work clothes seemed too large
for his body, as though he was embarrassed
by how his muscles bulged beneath
the red flannel shirt, top three buttons
missing, tails untucked from old jeans,
sleeves rolled halfway up his forearms hiding
most of the twin anchors tattooed there.

He has a yellow cedar board
in a vise & is running an old jack
plane down one edge. The blade is newly honed
& wood curls sweetly down the length
of each pass he leans his body into.

When the shop door opens, his wife
will speak to him without crossing
the sill. She will tell him she no longer
loves him, has not loved him for years. She will turn
& carry the full suitcase of her resentment
to the car it took them five years to pay for.
He will not see her again for six months.
He will lock the shop & let his tools rust.

For now he believes everything will be
all right if he can just cut away the high points,
square off the sides, sand this small board smooth.

Constellations

We knew he was different,
the one who called a pause
in our pasture baseball once,
the quiet, oldest son, still living
at home. He'd been to the store
& was taking a shortcut back. *Stop*,
he said, & we did, letting bats
& gloves dangle. *From this angle*
you could be . . . & he named
a constellation none of us knew
from school or Scouts. We were playing
work-up. I'd just hit an easy out
toward the cow flop we used for third,
a pop fly that rose like a soiled moon
before tumbling into the pocket
of Frankie's Ted Williams mitt
with a wet plop. That's when the man said
Stop, said we looked like stars in a field
of sky, said we should imagine each of us
a billion miles apart. For a moment
it scared us, so much sudden distance
from each flaring heart, & then
he shuffled away toward the sagging wire
fence, taking with him the Greek
name that for a moment helped him see
some sort of earthly sense.

Country Store

It wasn't the shiny shovels in a corner
bucket, bright kegs of nails, the smell
of new rope, or staples for the table
that had my attention, but the two shelves

under glass near the door & me with a nickel
in my pocket: wax lips, bubble gum
cigars, slices of sugared watermelon complete
with tiny seeds, wax bottles of syrup in four
flavors, laces of licorice, taffy, candy

cigarettes, fireballs, chocolate coins in gold
foil, jawbreakers, & they only cost a penny
apiece, a bribe for handing the owner a list
from my embarrassed mother—cheapest bread (two

loaves), a gallon of milk, a couple pounds
of bacon scraps, ten-pound sack of spuds—
&, please, could we pay at the end of the month,
hoping he'd say yes, we could, on account.

II

Inside the Body

My father is showing me secrets
inside the cavity of the buck
I've just shot, my first big kill. *Field dressing*
he calls it. He got me past the tongue
lolling like a slug alongside the mouth,
the open eyes, the broken BBs
of blood at the nostrils, by rolling the buck
on its back & having me clutch a fist of hair
& hide just above the crotch. He warns me to watch
for ticks, then makes the first careful cut
in the raised tent below my hand. When I let go,
he unzips the skin to the sternum, chops
through bone, cuts the windpipe
& yanks it back for a handle.

Now his forearms are red flags
in the deer's chest, his hands quick
& certain, unlatching the different parts,
naming them as they come: the halted muscle
of heart, liver, the flat lungs. He won't nick
the stomach, the bladder or gut, the small scent
gland. When the blade swerves toward the scrotum
my eyes flick away like nervous squirrels.

My father keeps his greatest scorn for anything
done *half-assed*. He is telling me,
with all the eloquence of his hands, that work
is bigger than I've thought. It's as near
as he can come to prayer for his son, though he

would never call it that, tilting the body
on its side so it all spills out onto
the frosty November grass.

What Was He Thinking, My Grandfather

when he reached across the front seat
of the car to offer me a drink—a snort

as he called it? There was always a bottle
in the glove box, cheap brandy to coddle

his habit, always in pints for the ease
of a pocket. I was six. He liked to tease,

so that's what I thought it was, at first. I knew he drank.
A separate can in the laundry shed clanked

with his empties. My grandmother only lowered
her head, thinned her lips. Their marriage had soured

years before. He drank while he drove, while he fished;
he drank while he mended his nets. I never saw him smashed

nor ever heard him slur his speech. He was a good
provider, brought most of his wages home, put food

on the table, paid his bills & salted some away.
He was a smart fisherman, sharp at business. Let no man say

he didn't make a good deal. Twelve years he'd swig,
then hold the bottle out to me in a fist as big

as the head of a sculpin, as though I hadn't heard
about occasional other women; how hard

he beat my father once; the whorehouse in Wrangall;
the time he stole a full load of kings from a single

fish trap & made it back with bullet holes
in the pilothouse, more in the starboard hull,

& no one ever said whether he'd fired
back; as though he knew I'd have to make hard

choices in my life, & I might as well get some practice,
might as well begin here, right now, with this.

Falling a Tree 90° to the Lean

for Lonnie

A Douglas fir, more than two feet
through, angled downslope,
having had to bend that way
for light. Blackcap & snow-
berry have been hacked back
from the base, salal stomped flat.
It smells of pitch, crushed nettles,
yesterday's rain. Our son has made
his undercut to the left
of the lean & knocked out
a chunk like a thick slab
of cake. He has started his back
cut, turned off the saw, & is pounding in
two plastic falling wedges
with the poll of his axe. His hard hat
is tilted back on his head. His forearms
are bare & scratched.

He is not thinking about
the smaller trees he would damage
should he take the easy fall,
the stumps that could shatter
good wood in the logs. He is paying
attention to the grudging give
of each wedge beneath his axe,
the sound it makes in the trunk,
how the crown shivers eighty
feet up. He is not thinking
how much simpler a winter cut

without the weight of spring
sap. He is imagining that first creak
as the hinge breaks, the tree
already on the ground. And, because
he is a father now, he has one wary eye
on the two routes of escape
he has carefully cut through
the brush. Some things are written
in the grain, he says, some hidden twist
in the fibers. Sometimes we need
to back away & simply let them
go, fall where they may.

Old Men on the Dock

Do they still come, spilling the catch
of their long lives, culling the dogfish & wolf
eels, jellyfish & sculpin from the money
fish, salmon in all of their guises?

In the off-season they'd scuffle along floats,
held up by knees that could no longer stand
a watch at the wheel, using pilings for balance,
creosote smeared on the sleeves of their tweed

coats; flannel & long johns beneath; a wool cap
with flaps for their ears; boots patched with gobs
of tar. We kept a chair or two on the dock
where the long black nets stretched out for mending,

the boat moored close, its fenders squeaking
lightly. There was always coffee
on the galley stove, a boy like me to fetch
thick cups that wouldn't break if dropped, a bottle

of whiskey for flavor. They hunched with a good knife
carving net needles from blanks
of yew. Much of the talk was sockeye & silvers,
humpies & kings, the names of points & bays,

best times to make a set, how to catch & use
a current that rose against underwater
cliffs. They talked tricks: how to live in the throb
of a diesel, ear tuned for a slur in its speech; how to think

like a fish; how to make gravy with cold coffee; keep
a straight wake with a hangover scraping barnacles
through the brain. They knew the names of friendly women
with houses in Juneau, Petersburg, Ketchikan.

They had been there, more salt in their socks
than our grannies had baked into bread. We knew
which questions brought stories: famous
storms; names of boats gone down, each crewman

lost; epic drunks; which skippers were sons
of bitches; what man stepped out for a piss
& vanished in a sudden roll or pitch; of salmon runs
so large that crows grew fat on the eyes

of the dead that dried on the banks. They spoke
around hand-rolled smokes, a pipe, a cheek
of snoose. The sound of each voice
was the hull of a skiff scraping

gravel. We listened, our hands wriggling at the nets,
searching out the rips, raveling, unraveling.

Shine

Christ, sonny, it's the what, not the who!
—Goody Matsen

I was nearly eighteen, between ships, moping
on the mess deck of Coast Guard Base
Seattle. Saturday night. I was broke
& alone when a retired gunny
from the Corps came in hoping
to sell insurance, but found only a half-full urn
of coffee & me putting a spit shine
on my liberty shoes. He poured a cup & sat
to give advice. Said I had a nice
technique but the water in my polishing lid
should be colder. Said the best was *ice-cold piss*
from a red-headed virgin. Said diaper squares
worked better than balls of cotton or scraps
from an old pair of skivvies. Said it was all
about layering the wax. Said I should keep
a light touch: *Imagine you're making slow circles*
around a woman's belly button. When at last
I set the shoes on the table, the toecaps
gleamed. He said they were about right,
that I should be able to stand beside
the captain's wife, look at my toes,
& say what color panties she'd picked
that day. I started to put away my gear.
He put a hand on my wrist. *What about the backs?*
No one, I said, did those, because the pants hung low
enough to cover. He said, *Listen, kid. A man*
who doesn't shine the backs of his shoes is a man
who doesn't wipe his ass. I did the backs,
said thanks, said how squared away
I'd look. He scraped his chair back,

gave me his card, said some day
I might need insurance more than cash. Said
I might have made a marine. Said, *Two things.*
You don't brag just because you wiped your ass.
And you don't shine your shoes so you'll *look good,*
you do it so somebody else *will wanna look good.*
The miracle was I understood.

Knots

I learned my Latin & Greek from the sharp edge
of my master's stick & the leather strap of his scorn.
—C. F. Hoyt

In boot camp, far from hometown
schools & my mother's kitchen, I learned to tell
a square knot from a granny, my teacher
six & a half feet of muscled bosun arched
above my five feet two, my hands palsied
in the hurricane of his voice. I was:
dickhead, shit-for-brains, dumb-ass, fuzz
nuts. I was *lower than whale shit on the bottom*
of the ocean. He threatened to use my head
for a holystone if I didn't get my whippings
right. *My daughter's got bigger hands. You sure*
you ain't a girl? Pay attention, numb nuts. This here
is how to tie a bowline. None of that silly rabbit shit
you heard in Scouts. Make a bight in the line
with your left hand & take the running end
in your right. Here's how you remember: Your pecker
sticks up through a hatch in the deck, then snakes
around the mast looking for the bung hole
in a barrel, but there's the bosun on watch, so it slides
itself back down the hatch, cinches tight, & dangles
there. Got it? I learned two stopper
hitches, half hitch, round hitch, sheepshank,
reef knot. *How can you be so clumsy, kid?*
This ain't for a merit badge. You wanna lose
good government gear? Get a shipmate hurt or dumped
over the side? You want to embarrass *me, boy?* Eye
splice, long splice, short splice, back splice—
That's called a dog splice, too, turd. You know why? 'Cuz
it looks like a dog's dick. And if you don't trim away
those Irish pennants, I'm gonna beat you

into jellyfish with it. He taught us nothing
fancy, no monkey's fist, sinnets or
Turk's-Heads. *These are knots for working
sailors, pissant, not weekend boaters* each stressed
syllable a slap of my starched white hat
across my beardless face
with his big black hand again & again
until he was satisfied. Forty-five years,
& I still can tie a bowline one-handed,
pick my way through nearly any chore
worth doing, strand by stubborn strand, right
to the bitter end.

Working with Hayden Carruth
(1921-2008)

Come work with me awhile, Hayden,
I can use your company in the shed
among tools your hands have never lost
remembrance for. This jack plane was a gift
from Sally's father, a man who made his own tools
when he had to. I've had it more than 30 years.
Don't wince at the rust. On this island
the air seems always damp. The iron needs
an edge. We flip the lever cap, slide the pieces
off the frog, & use a quarter to loosen the screw
that holds the clamp. Who taught you,
Hayden? I learned from Mr. Baldwin,
my high school shop teacher, who wore loud bow ties
& grieved his way through tough & troubled kids.
We start with a coarse stone & a little light
oil. I use a guide I found on a yard sale table
on the mainland to keep the blade atilt at 30°. Against
all logic to push it forward instead of pulling back,
but it works, the sound a bit like something dragged
across a concrete floor. A dozen strokes, a dozen more,
& then we switch to the harder stone to wear away
the burr. Arkansas' best. I learned to check an edge
against the nail of my thumb. Just drop, & see if it snags
or simply slides away. Setting the blade back in the throat
is always hit or miss. Expose too much
& gouge the wood; too little brings an empty
rattle. We want that perfect curl, the sole gliding
with the grain, the saw marks giving up, knots
like small exploding novas. You know it, that slight good

ache in the elbow, the shoulder turning with the hip,
the soft *shush* & *shush* like soothing a fussy child.
You can work till the heel of your hand hurts & sweat
stains the wood. There's a stack of cedar boards
stickered a dozen paces from this shed. I love the smell
of cedar when it's planed, so sharp it burns
the nose, then dances across the tongue. The boards
will have to wait. A coat of oil against the wet,
& the plane goes back on its shelf. Just maintenance,
Hayden. Busy work, a bit of labor to push aside
the fear of you sick again, as though imagining your hands
on mine could somehow hold you here, as though
it's enough, the basic lesson I've learned from you:
The job's not done until it's square, & level, & true.

III

Small Noticings

The last of the figs
has already dropped
when I go out to pick it
for breakfast. By the time
I scrape off the red ants
& a single black slug, the small
scrap left is sweeter
than a whole fig sliced
on a white plate.

Rain batters leaves on the berry bushes,
the lilac drips, my grandmother's rose
is a sorry, sorry worker in the wet.
For the fire in the stove, *thanks.* For dry wood
beneath the blue tarps, *thanks.* For coffee
warming my hands, the raincoat I found
in the island rummage when we had no money,
& for the gift of leaving it on its hook
today, *praise & thanks, thanks & praise.*

The sound of cedar splitting
under the axe
is its own reward.

Bring in a load of wood
& stack it in the basket. A wasp
slides from a crack in a chunk
of white fir & lies curled
on the tiled hearth, a queen
whose whole life is a dream
of next spring. When she stirs
in the house heat, we'll have to choose
between fire & chance.

Another dead rat on the rug
by the stove this morning. In my bare
feet I nearly step on it. Flattened.
Paws reaching. One of its bared
teeth chipped. A flea jumps
off when I lift with a gloved hand,
its leap a kind of belief.

Yellow jasmine blooming
in the yard a month early, brighter
than new butter in this washed-out
day. A single sprig on top
the piano lightens
the burden of weather
inside & out.

Morning coffee in the dark. All
the demands of the day light
like crows weighting the limbs
of a cedar, one, then two, & another,
until the tree is freighted with black
shapes, all squawking
at once.

A small moth flutters up from the covers
on my bed & scribes the entire text
of its life in the air before stalling
in the mouth of the lamp chimney
where it becomes a brief flare,
an unexpected flourish.

There were large alders there
& there. Two cedars
by the woodpile, a hemlock
near the compost. A Doug fir
& two old white fir,
those three big stumps.
In twenty years we've pushed
the forest back. What light we have
has come at cost & slowly.
Always we live in the shadows
of the dead.

In the upturned cap
of a mushroom; the split lip
of a tossed tomato; in the shell
of a cracked egg in the compost;
the dimple of a maple leaf;
in a small crack in the handle
of a hoe on its side; the eye
sockets of a dead thrush, its slightly
parted beak; in every hollow space
exposed to weather, rain
come to this stillness.

All night the beans soaked
in water we pumped from the well.
All day they've simmered
in a pot on the back of the cookstove
with only a bay leaf for spice. Red
beans. Lift the lid & the whole house
thickens. Soup & bread & a mug
of cold water will be enough. That swallows
are playing in the yard outside
the kitchen window is just dessert.

These yellow flowers in the yard
just four days after mowing
aren't dandelions, but Hairy Cats Ear.
How would you feel taking a sickle
& walking across the grass toward a weed
with a name that says it hears
you're coming?

A robin announces the first elderberry
blossoms, singing from a fat branch
as though the blooms were already
berries, the berries already fermented,
the robin already drunk & dreading
the long hangover of winter.

Sharpen the saw, fall & buck
two maples shading
the row of Marion berries. Cut
a dead stand of wild filbert
into lengths for the kitchen
range. Come into the house smelling
of mixed gas, bar oil &
next winter's apple pie.

That quick flick of feathers
in the elderberry, shudder of blossom
in the plum, high, then lowest
branch, then back, then front, then only
a wrong patch of color in the salmonberry, twitch
among leaves & canes, turns out,
she says, after half an hour with field guides,
to be a solitary vireo. Perhaps.

Wild bees have made a nest
in the hot tub stove. The metal
jacket vibrates with their buzz,
travelers exchanging news, lovers
elaborating techniques,
the sweet uses of the tongue.

Hard to stack wood & live
in the moment. The body knows
the picking & spacing & wedging
to make the stack right. The mind is in
December by a good fire, soup
simmering on the back
of the stove, coffee dark
as winter nights, & the sound
of a six-day rain on tarps
over the woodpile.

After splitting the last
of the small rounds for the kitchen
range, two mounds as high
as my waist; after bucking the last
of the alder; after stowing
the saws & cleaning the chips
from the ragged cuffs of my pants,
the oil & grime from my face,
rinsing sawdust from my hair:
fresh raspberries from the garden
in a blue-glazed bowl.

A shadow drifts over
the clearing, striping
a small fir in its passing.
The tiger cat curled by the lilac
looks up; the tabby under
a rhubarb leaf looks up
briefly; the rabbit by the rose
shuts down, becomes wood,
stares at nothing
that might remind it
what it is.

On the binding table, a hundred-
year-old book of Irish verse. Five minutes
to take apart, failed glue & rotten thread
removed. Five hours to make it whole,
new boards, bright cloth, the joys & griefs
of old harpers still singing.

IV

After the Argument

He spent the afternoon pulling nails
from salvaged boards. Each yank
of the crowbar brought a scream
from the wood. Then he hammered them
on a chunk of railroad steel,
threw them into a coffee can
on the workbench, knowing
they were straight, merely by the feel.

"Snail, Snail, Glister Me Forward"

—Theodore Roethke

The wet track of this snail across an alder leaf
is so like my slow tongue on her thigh.
Except I can't tell where the snail paused.
Or for how long. Or why.

Lady Slipper

This one is ten feet off the trail,
an inch from where I set down my saw,
the color of a girl's most earnest
blush, open, as she might open her lips
in mute surprise. Some call it
"Calypso," after the nymph who kept a man
seven years from his wife with the magic
of her body in bed, Greek for *hidden*.

Pick it & the plant will not bloom
again. Dig it up & it will die
away from where it was rooted.

Forgive me if all I bring you
is its name & the brief story
of how it stands in a patch of moss
swept clean in a small wash
of light no larger than a sole
into which we push with care
the small, perfectly fitting foot of love.

Tulip Field, McLean Road

If there were a single word
for the color of these tulips,
it would have to contain
the bright swirl of my mother's favorite
skirt. She square-danced in it for years, until
some inner joy faded faster than the fabric.
It would need to have the scarlet
of a single maple leaf
caught in a spider's web between
two trees in the orchard
my wife & I planted
together. And the splendor of an apple
polished on the wool of a Pendleton
shirt my grandfather left
a little wear in when he died.

I say *red* & want to hold it
with my tongue longer than teeth
& gums will let me—
skirt & *leaf, shirt* & *apple*—
& no lexicon to help me.

UHTCEARU: Morning Sorrow
La Conner, Washington, May 2010

for Sally & 40 years

A red-winged blackbird is calling from a green
puzzle of leaves beside the back door
of this house where I've borrowed
a room, his song floating from the bush
across razor grass & drift to the Channel's edge.
Tide is flooding north. Sun just sliding
above the mountains, a bright blade of light
that can't quite match the slash
of color on the bird's wing. *O-ka-lee*
it sings, *o-ka-lee*, flinging the sound like joy
toward whatever might be listening,
& I am away from you again, whispering
back this ancient Anglo-Saxon word.

Botanical

Maybe, at some stage, love includes kneeling
in dungarees beside the long-time beloved
at a stem of Queen Anne's lace, taking the time
to dig up a portion of the root, peel it
for the carroty smell, point out the umbels
that form a cup like the nest of a small bird,
a single central flower the red of a ruby or a drop
of the queen's own blood, how the leaves are like lace.

And maybe love includes kneeling again alongside
a stalk of Yarrow near where the neighbor's goats
are tied, the tiny white clusters of blossoms different,
you tell him, one old hand guiding the tips of his
fingers to the shape of the leaves, their give &
bending—*plumajillo,* "soft feathers,"—telling the tale
of Achilles tending the hurts of his warriors
with a clever poultice. *Staunchweed,* you say. *Woundwort.*

And maybe this long love contains the nearly certain
knowledge that the beloved, though he vows this time
to remember, might, in a week, mistake one plant
for the other as he has for more than forty years,
such love tenacious as any weed we might describe,
but cannot always name.

Slow Air

for Sally

Not a jig, not a reel,
but a tune for a fiddler
with a country heart,
a feel for the pace
of figs coming ripe
in the orchard, the rising
of smoke from a thousand
winter fires,
the lazy gestures
of laundry on the line,
bedding & work clothes,
practical flannel,
of chore boots waiting
by the door to the mudroom,
of two-day soup
on top the cookstove,
of tea water calling
a boil, a life here
simple as slipping
the belt from your robe,
the body still willing
though muscles are aching,
we lead & we follow,
the tune still a-making.

Daffodils This Time, McLean Road Again

All week children in the schools I visit
try to help me with *yellow.* How do I tell
my wife, back home on our island,
what it's like? *Take a picture,* says one. No,
I say, what *I* see, not what the camera sees.

Es un amarillo tan brillante, says a girl, like butter
mi abuela melts on my toast. No,
says another, like the raincoat my father wears
in the fields. Maybe the lemon my mother slices
for shrimp soup. *Los ojos de nuestro perro,* those old
doggy eyes in the porch light. Ripe corn just shucked.
La camisa de Mr. Shapiro, or Ms. Romero's pencil.
The way my mother laughs. The stripes
on a wasp, the one that stung me. A banana,
says another, because I'm hungry.

But I am thinking of the yellow lunchbox
I lost when I was nine working in the berry fields. Inside,
on sheets of paper, was the name of a girl written
two hundred precise times, a charm to make her love me
back. I never spoke to her again, afraid someone
found it & told. Ten times ten
thousand flowers, the color of absence,
silent, forthright, cold.

V

Roadside Event

A wild rhododendron explodes
from the open hood
of an old Ford truck
& not one bystander
is injured anywhere but in
the stubborn, unarmored heart.

Missing

for K.A., vanished January 2010

After a full day scanning
the parking lot of every church,
tavern, supermarket, neighborhood
store, motel, hotel, restaurant,
drive-in, gas station, park,
trailhead, taping flyers to doors,
that face I knew for fifty years,
driving the back route to Sultan,
534 east to Highway 9, southeast & east
again on 2; after checking the gravel
at the road's edge wherever
there was a ravine & no guard-
rail, getting out a dozen times
to walk back, look close & closer
through salmonberry, vine
maple, ocean spray, Nootka
rose; after heading back in reverse,
picking up the Old Pacific
& Pioneer Highways, finding only
three trucks the color of his in 200
miles, right year, but the wrong plates,
I parked myself, finally, off the road
by a field near Fir Island
to watch a thousand snow geese lift
from the stubble, drift, & fall again
like ash into rain shine, wondering
how many geese are lost
each year to coyotes, hunters, feral
dogs & boys with .22s, & whether any goose
might miss another voice among so many

wild voices, one shape among such common
shapes, there are so many there to lose.

Sighting

There was disagreement about the color.
Like dried blood on a barn board,
said one. Brighter, said another,
like a berry just before it ripens.

No one claimed to see the whole
of it, just a patch of fur through Oregon
grape or salal, a blur, like the swirl
of a goldfish in muddy water.

There had to be doubters,
those who thought it might have been an otter
or a muskrat chased from its pond.
So improbable, a fox

on our tiny island, harsh currents
on all sides, cold northwest water & miles
to the mainland. No one had lost
a chicken. No scat that couldn't be identified.

For weeks we walked the tideline
scanning wet sand for tracks, stayed alert
on every trail, the edges of fields, gardens,
the long boundary of the gravel airstrip.

Each least leaf was more cleanly itself,
everything brightened while we strained
to see something the color of rust
in the bottom of a bucket, or of coals in a stove
still hot enough to be dangerous.

Calling the Old Dog In

for Jerry & Kathy

It's no good standing on the porch
& yelling. He's deaf
as a man with long years
in the engine room of a ship listening

for the sounds metal makes
before it fails, a faint break
in rhythm, something out of tune.
He is lying in the middle

of the road, staring east
across a field of pumpkins
ruined by the cold.
He can't hear ducks or geese

resting in the marsh talking one another
through the night in comfort
or complaint. Or coyotes
barking across the Valley.

Traffic is far away, only a whisper,
like blood through a vein.
Some dark scent, perhaps, tugs
his head back & forth
in an old, old way.

If he hears anything, it is likely the light
beating in his chest, already diminishing,
though neither of us knows it.
He is sprawled in a black bed

of glittering frost,
so that I wonder if he's had to lie down
to keep from falling into the sea
of stars above him. When he turns

his head at my touch
his eyes fill with a small joy,
as though love is so easily given
even I might as well have a little,

as though, when he rises
& trots toward the house
& his bed,
I needn't follow after.

Mixing Concrete

is mostly a matter of keeping simple count:
ten shovels of gravel hauled from the beach,
eight of sand taken from that pit by the island
airstrip, all shoveled from separate mounds
on a blue tarp & tossed in the mixer with half a bag
of Portland cement. Rest, & count the crows

flapping from a cedar, count the early apples coming
ripe on the tree by the old cabin, the five neighbors
giving a day for bowls of soup & beer,
the single cat prowling the forms. Add six quarts
of water, the other half bag of cement,
gravel, sand again. All that is easy. It's water

that's mystical. Five gallons to a sack is the model,
depending how wet the aggregate, whether
it's raining. How hard. Too wet, & the mix just
splashes, falls like thin mud; too dry, & it crumbles or sticks
to the sides of the mixer. What you want is a sort of wave
breaking over the blades, peeling from the drum

as it tumbles. At some point even a little spit could turn it
too wet, & the foreman will leave the forms to complain.
Everyone has a secret way to know when it's right: some
by squeezing, some by the weight in an overturned
palm, some by smell, some by the sound of it sloughing.
Each load is its own problem until it's poured

into waiting barrows, half a mixer load
in each, shivering as it levels. But say, after nine hours

of labor, you lift the shovel from gravel & spot, mid-swing,
the off-white of bone, the right foreleg from a drowned
deer, a chip in the outer edge of its hoof? A doe
by the shape. What do you do, shovel quivering

at the end of your cramping arms, the southwest end
of the foundation in view, & the sudden vision of a house,
light among the trees, just on the verge of rising?

Reading the Stumps

Our son says it's how he went
to school, prowling the woods where
work was done for logs instead

of fields. It's all there, he says, how the faller
moved from step to step. Look for the pinch
of the saw where the trunk settled away

from the hinge, marks left by the bar
& chain pressed into the wood. Check
the level of the face cut against the back.

Too high? Low? How much wood
left in the hinge? Did it break
too soon or late? Check the rings

for a clue to the lean: wider growth
on one side means it went that way
for light. Wedge marks? How far in

& how many? How sharp was the chain?
Any hesitation cuts? He learns a bit
from each mistake, admires the ones who knew

their jobs, each stump a signature
to their work. That's what he wants,
he says, not his name, but his mark.

Checking the Boat at Night in a Storm

Because anchors let go their grip,
shackles wear, lines part, you rise when wind
becomes too loud to bear & slide out of bed
without waking your wife.

Because your wife still sleeps you dress
without light by the kitchen door, chore
boots & oilskins, watch cap & gloves,
& let yourself out into the dark.

Because it's dark, you carry
an old-fashioned lantern, the squeak
of its handle lost in gusts that sound
like runaway trucks, the harsh cracks
of limbs giving up, letting go.

Because limbs are tumbling
onto roads & trails,
you should not take the shortcut
through the timber, but you do,
pushing the small pool of light
before you, eyes on the muddy duff,
crawling under one windfall fir
& the fresh wreck of an old madrone
until rain becomes a sideways slash.

Because the rain hits your face
full-on, you know you're out
of the woods beside Phil's hay-
field, & you lean into the storm downhill

to find the old road that follows the bluff
above the dark bulk of the bay,
the pounding of breakers loud
now as wind, metallic shriek of the ramp
pitching as the float bucks & slams into pilings
at the county dock, beside which you stop,
water breaking to the tops of your boots
before sucking the loose pebbles back.

Because everything is down to a few shades
of black, it does no good to look. A hundred yards
offshore your dory is riding the swells like a gull
as they roll beneath it, or it is already
kindling farther up the beach.

This is what you know: you filed the bow
thimble clean, made the eye splice tight.
In scuba gear you set the anchor yourself
in the muddy bottom, a Danforth, flukes
dug in, shaft facing the shore, tightened
the shackle pins, checked each link
of the chain to the nylon line, left plenty of scope
for tide or weather, kept it clean of mussels
& seaweed. The buoy was firm & floated high.
Your painter was new, strong, & tied with a bowline.

You knew all this before you left your bed—
that all that might be done you did. Yet here you are,
holding watch where you can't tell wind from surf,
salt spray from rain. Because. Because. Because again.

Watching My Neighbor on the Dock

Behind him, across the bay's bight, trees
have left a scar on the bank after a slide. A cat's-
paw stirs the water. My neighbor is standing on heart-

wood beams milled from island timber, the hard hearts
of firs that logged a hundred years against wind, their rings a poetry
of weathered remembrance. I see him slide his phone into the catch

of his pocket & turn to the lines of his boat, their catalog
of knots. Two are too taut, another too slack. Enough art
in that work to distract. He has just entered the country

of cancer, compass out of true, caught without a chart.

Gooseberry

At night, when we sleep,
something eats the leaves
of the gooseberry, leaves them
ragged, like the edges of pages
torn from a church hymnal.

It is some hidden worm, we guess,
but the soil at its base
yields nothing, nothing shows
in the glare of the flashlight after dark.

Each day the green edges recede,
until only thc ridiculous thorns
are left threatening the air.

We try diatomaceous earth, tanglefoot,
powders & sprays, remove the fallen
leaves & re-till the ground around
the trunk. Carbolic acid doesn't work,
nor foxglove infusions, nor offhanded
prayer. What we know is something
needs a care we cannot measure
up to. Something else works in the dark,
more patient, more hungry, more sure.

Walking in Place, Waldron Island

I love to walk a leisure hour
A distance from the town
—John Clare

After three months in a mainland city
it's good to be back to this four & a half
square miles, a hundred folk, & the joke is
that I haven't seen a single soul

in two hours of walking trails & roads.
I hear their saws, their chickens, dogs
& doors. They are busy with chores,
no doubt, inside & out of their cabins

& houses. I haven't heard a car
alarm in days. One of the ways
we know who we are is by reciting
lists of what we love, like Clare

across his fields. I love the loons
in North Bay, & the way herring gulls
sound like small children playing
at games. Nettles are coming up, high

as my knees already. The hummers
are back, an unlikely blur in the blooms
of wild currant. I love the smell of wood
smoke, a neighbor's lights shimmering

through trees like fish scales, the sound
of frogs from the Adams' two ponds. I am
a long distance from town, walking,
as though I could walk myself home.

for Tony Curtis

Cist, National Museum, Dublin

She is folded into a square
of stones the way a child might squeeze
herself into her mother's drawer
in a game of hide & seek, or the way
another might tuck herself under
a blanket too small for her, the night
cold & long. Her stillness is casual,
like a chair put away after summer,
or into a closet after church
coffee & cake. And yet nothing
is connected: each vertebra is a pilgrim
who has given up & sprawled
in a long arc on the bank of a dry river;
the clever puzzle of her ribs is collapsed
like a basket left too long in the yard.
Each brown bone is light as a bird's least
intention. The clay bowl beside her head
is a well of stale air. Absurd to think
we could fill it with anything meaningful:
the heavy coin of embarrassment, the paper
currency of prayer. Four thousand years confined
to her room. If we lifted the glass from her tomb,
slid away the cover, we could hear the slow
sound of atoms waving farewell.

Exercise Yard, Kilmainham Gaol

We've already seen the other highlights: the beam
above the main door where men were left
hanging; the five carved snakes; the cells; the chapel
where Plunkett was married just hours before death.

This is where men broke stones
the size of melons into gravel, each blow
a prayer, or curse. Under the grim ballistics of rain,
we learn these facts:
that cross marks the spot where Connolly died, tied
to his chair. The rest were shot on the other side.
The stone walls are bare. Not even lichen grows here.
An Irish flag droops from its pole, limp as a sole
in the bottom of a dory. Our guide wants out
of the rain, hurries the story, & leads us away
from the yard. A rook flaps
heavily overhead. One old man lags
behind, turns to the wall, leans into it, & drags
his left palm—slowly—against a patch
of mortar gray as an old scrap of sheet.
Leaves blood. Turns his hand to look
at the scraped lines in the skin.
Nods. Pauses. Nods again.

Wine-Dark Sea

for Paula Meehan

Ah, there it is! Just as you said,
the color of strong Samos wine,
dark as blood on a stone,
not the deep blue of the day, the turquoise
of shallows. Chips of stars, a thin tiara
of moon—as much as might show
in a girl's thick hair. It's what Orestes
must have seen when he raised the temple
up the hill to Artemis, almost believing
a man might drink & drink & still
contrive to make it home.

Good Friday Epitafios, Panaghia Kimitirion, Island of Patmos

So that's where the swallows are nesting,
under an arch above the outer narthex.
We wondered where, all these swallows
embroidering the sky. The priest is singing
the ritual directly below the nest. The rest
of us have spilled out into the courtyard waiting
the body of Christ, wrapped in its shrouds,
to be brought out & borne through the stone
streets while we follow with our sad
brown candles. The nervous parents flick
in & out of the light from the church. In this wind
we cannot even keep our candles lit.

VI

Diagnosis

for the opening of the new Cancer Treatment
& Wellness Center, Renton, Washington

My mother said it was like having a stray
dog appear at her heels, a shadow,
unpredictable as any strange
animal in the neighborhood. Sometimes
she could hear it breathing quietly,
sometimes a restless growl in the throat.
Once it came, it never wholly went away.

It followed closest those days she gave her body up
to the care of others, room by room, secret
by secret, a world of needles, numbers & shiny
inexplicable machines. She felt, she said,
like a puzzle spilled onto someone else's floor.

I wanted to know what pulled her through.
She said that none of her doctors pretended. They knew
what walked beside her, & let her know they knew.
One by one, they helped her turn the pieces
round until she recognized herself again.

And something else, for which she had no
words. I think she wanted to say how hope
fluttered around her head like a small flock of birds
come in through an open window out of the cold.
Day after day she listened to their changing song
through all her doctors' care, the staff's regard,
her husband's patient tending:

mistake   a cure   remission   more time   less pain

My mother kept her eyes on those fragile wings stitching
together fragments of light, turning & turning
just out of reach of the dog's mouth, its sudden bite.

Spring Elegy

for Mary Skinner's Memorial, Yakima, 2009

Now someone will have to be
less careful with a lie,
someone else can feel more free
to turn away an eye
from what is wrong.
Some child's hope can come unstrung
now that she is gone,
unless we say
hers was a good life,
hers was a right way.
Although we cannot stand
exactly as she stood,
we still can honor what she would,
we still can act as one
to uphold what she did,
to grieve & move ahead
with what she left undone,
& what she left unsaid.

Hometown Park

for the opening of the new children's playground,
Storvik Park, Anacortes, Washington

That crow, if there were wind,
might be a kite. Daisies are only white
until the mower comes again.

That child whining for a turn
on the slide could be yours,
or could be you, enough years gone.

That old woman who slid a stone
into her sweater pocket will take it out
& rub it with her thumb when she's alone.

That dry complaint is creaking swings.
A mother laughs & pushes.
Her daughter shouts & sings.

There, some boy counted the loose
change of love into a girl's hand, a ring
gathered & bent the light of stars onto grass.

There, a son collapsed on the damp seat
of a bench having said good-bye
at the funeral home across the street.

Here is where a gray dog decided not to bark.
He lies beside his gray master & listens
to the town grow quiet in the coming dark.

There's always more than one way in. Come. Stay
long enough to know what brought you here,
what you leave behind, what you take away.

Closing the Art School

Spokane, 2008

Is it enough one woman recalls
the way light rolled off the glaze
of a cup lifted warm from the kiln,
how it matched the precise shade
of lipstick worn by her mother
in the '40s, a permanent blessing
on the cup's rim?

Is it enough another can describe
how the smell of paint thinner brings back
that moment when a classmate confessed
his shy desire not to paint geese, or even the flight
of geese, but the intimate specificity
of emotion the first time he remembered
hearing a flock pass overhead, their joyful
noise louder than his parents' argument?

Is it enough a woman admits
she was bored with talk
of shading, the subtle suggestion
of lines, until she found, in the corner
of a drawing in her sketchbook,
some marks suggesting the features
of her absent father's face,
how shocked she was to find him
softer than she remembered?

Is it enough that couple fell in love
throwing pots together, left streaks
of wet clay on one another's bodies,
shared wedding wine from goblets
the color of freshly turned earth?

Is it enough a woman's hands coaxed
the color of violence from random scraps
of cloth, though the needle stuttered
& shook in her fingers,
but steadied each time she took a stitch, until
finally she sewed herself back together?

Is it enough this man knows of a single painting
left by a woman cancer took in a rush, how it daily
invents the house it inhabits, a woman, he says,
whose two crooked fingers she trained
to hold a brush?

Is it enough that 40 years of students
could mind how colors aren't just pine
pollen, basalt, or wheat, but also the dazzle
of grass after rain, the breath of a deer lifting
its muzzle from the edge of a lake?

Is it enough they will always know, unmistakably,
the sound of a palette knife scraping canvas,
the smell of wet boar bristles, the snap
of beads on strings, the rap
of a mallet & chisel on wood, on stone?

We hope it's enough, this necessary shattering
of the self that moves us forward,
even as we mourn.

What We Carry on the Trail

for the dedication of the Vancouver Land Bridge,
Confluence Project, August 2008

We know that Lewis saw the hoary aster. He left
a sketch & kept a sample pressed & dried
like something in a card sent back
from holy lands by some devoted uncle.

We know how well he kept his watch.
No doubt he heard the hiss of water
over sand, of fur sliding through an ocean
of grass, & knew the difference. All day he cast
the heavy net of his attention & sorted the catch
at night: the size & shape of a grizzly's track,
the raucous calls of geese & ducks. He ground
ink, mixed colors, & left his mark. At times
his notebooks seem to fear
the awful abundance of things.

We know he never saw salt cedar,
Russian olive, the ruthless canes
of Himalayan blackberry.
They came, like us, later.

We don't know whether he noticed
a certain lupine. Had it been in bloom
it would have seemed just one more patch
of color on the spread quilt of the day,
something to remind him
of his sister's bonnet, his mother's apron,
or laundry drying on a neighbor's line.

He might have picked a stalk to count
its nodes or tally its tight buds
the way a man at rest might finger wet stones
after rain, or pick & chew a stem of grass.
He might have seen cocoons
hidden in the leaves. A few weeks more
& a butterfly, blue as trade beads or prairie sky,
would have been riding the breeze,
dependent on this single plant.

He could not have known how rare
that lupine would become,
how trained dogs would come
to hunt it by scent, how every year it blooms
more near the abrupt cliff
of absence. If wild bees hummed
prayers, they might contain the names
of flowers in trouble.

Like Lewis, like Clark, we have set our feet
on a bridge into the future, intending to arrive
with everything we've come to love—including
the brown pelican, Kincaid's lupine,
Fender's blue butterfly. We teach our children
each step is a name that matters.

We have traveled a long, long way & are traveling
still. We carry the cost of failure, the lengthening list
of what is gone already, of all that might be lost, knowing
what we have to do, not knowing if we will.

What the Culinary Arts Teacher Knows About Grace

for Georgia Johnson

It is there, she thinks, in the way cookies slip
from a greased pan, still limp
with the heat of the oven, chocolate chip,
music on the radio, a student's body moving
with the beat; in the scent of coriander
on a girl's palms, the print of her thumbs
at the edges of dough, *samosas* taking shape, each
the size of a bite, the way desire is measured.
She thinks of grace in the sound of a heavy knife
in a boy's hand slicing the skin
of a salmon, slabs of pink meat
laid out on the smokehouse racks, the heat
of alder coals, smoke turning flesh sweet
as sugar spilled into coffee the workers drink
to stay awake; in the long, thin strands
of pasta steaming on a white plate, the freight
of red sauce heavy with basil & oregano, allspice,
garlic & the white crystals of salt, of soft
bread stained with butter. Grace in the soup
zapped in a blue bowl laced with *Tapatío*
& lime, tortillas rolled with the weight
of a mother's whole life behind her & fried
crisp. It's in the chancy edges of knives,
forks with bent tines, the tarnished handles
of spoons that strike the side of a bowl
with a joyous sound. What daily saves her is the grace
that includes these hands, the ones that reach,
that gratefully receive, that pass the gift around.

Recent titles in the Carnegie Mellon Poetry Series

2002
Keeping Time, Suzanne Cleary
Astronaut, Brian Henry
What it Wasn't, Laura Kasischke
Slow Risen Among the Smoke Trees, Elizabeth Kirschner
The Finger Bone, Kevin Prufer
Among the Musk Ox People, Mary Ruefle
The Late World, Arthur Smith

2003
Trouble, Mary Baine Campbell
A Place Made of Starlight, Peter Cooley
Taking Down the Angel, Jeff Friedman
Lives of Water, John Hoppenthaler
Imitation of Life, Allison Joseph
Except for One Obscene Brushstroke, Dzvinia Orlowsky
The Mastery Impulse, Ricardo Pau-Llosa
Casino of the Sun, Jerry Williams

2004
The Women Who Loved Elvis All Their Lives, Fleda Brown
The Chronic Liar Buys a Canary, Elizabeth Edwards
Freeways and Aqueducts, James Harms
Prague Winter, Richard Katrovas
Trains in Winter, Jay Meek
Tristimania, Mary Ruefle
Venus Examines Her Breast, Maureen Seaton
Various Orbits, Thom Ward

2005
Things I Can't Tell You, Michael Dennis Browne
Bent to the Earth, Blas Manuel De Luna

Blindsight, Carol Hamilton
Fallen from a Chariot, Kevin Prufer
Needlegrass, Dennis Sampson
Laws of My Nature, Margot Schilpp
Sleeping Woman, Herbert Scott
Renovation, Jeffrey Thomson

2006
Burn the Field, Amy Beeder
The Sadness of Others, Hayan Charara
A Grammar to Waking, Nancy Eimers
Dog Star Delicatessen: New and Selected Poems 1979–2006, Mekeel McBride
Shinemaster, Michael McFee
Eastern Mountain Time, Joyce Peseroff
Dragging the Lake, Robert Thomas

2007
Trick Pear, Suzanne Cleary
So I Will Till the Ground, Gregory Djanikian
Black Threads, Jeff Friedman
Drift and Pulse, Kathleen Halme
The Playhouse Near Dark, Elizabeth Holmes
On the Vanishing of Large Creatures, Susan Hutton
One Season Behind, Sarah Rosenblatt
Indeed I Was Pleased with the World, Mary Ruefle
The Situation, John Skoyles

2008
The Grace of Necessity, Samuel Green
After West, James Harms
Anticipate the Coming Reservoir, John Hoppenthaler
Convertible Night, Flurry of Stones, Dzvinia Orlowsky
Parable Hunter, Ricardo Pau-Llosa
The Book of Sleep, Eleanor Stanford

2009
Divine Margins, Peter Cooley
Cultural Studies, Kevin A. González
Dear Apocalypse, K. A. Hays
Warhol-o-rama, Peter Oresick
Cave of the Yellow Volkswagen, Maureen Seaton
Group Portrait from Hell, David Schloss
Birdwatching in Wartime, Jeffrey Thomson

2010
The Diminishing House, Nicky Beer
A World Remembered, T. Alan Broughton
Say Sand, Daniel Coudriet
Knock Knock, Heather Hartley
In the Land We Imagined Ourselves, Jonathan Johnson
Selected Early Poems: 1958-1983, Greg Kuzma
The Other Life: Selected Poems, Herbert Scott
Admission, Jerry Williams

2011
Having a Little Talk with Capital P Poetry, Jim Daniels
Oz, Nancy Eimers
Working in Flour, Jeff Friedman
Scorpio Rising: Selected Poems, Richard Katrovas
The Politics, Benjamin Paloff
Copperhead, Rachel Richardson

2012
Now Make an Altar, Amy Beeder
Still Some Cake, James Cummins
Comet Scar, James Harms
Early Creatures, Native Gods, K. A. Hays
That Was Oasis, Michael McFee
Blue Rust, Joseph Millar

Spitshine, Anne Marie Rooney
Civil Twilight, Margot Schilpp

2013
Oregon, Henry Carlile
Selvage, Donna Johnson
At the Autopsy of Vaslav Nijinksy, Bridget Lowe
Silvertone, Dzvinia Orlowsky
Fibonacci Batman: New & Selected Poems (1991-2011),
    Maureen Seaton
When We Were Cherished, Eve Shelnutt
The Fortunate Era, Arthur Smith
Birds of the Air, David Yezzi

2014
Night Bus to the Afterlife, Peter Cooley
Alexandria, Jasmine Bailey
Dear Gravity, Gregory Djanikian
Pretenders, Jeff Friedman
How I Went Red, Maggie Glover
All That Might Be Done, Samuel Green
Man, Ricardo Pau-Llosa
The Wingless, Cecilia Llompart